Special Education Teacher Planner

SELF PUBLISHED BY AMAZON KINDLE DIRECT PUBLISHING

HTTPS://WWW.TEACHERSPAYTEACHERS.COM/STORE/LIVE-WIRE-LEARNER-SPECIAL-EDUCATION

COVER DESIGN BY CANVA

ISBN: 9798877661370

FIRST EDITION: JANUARY 27, 2024

PRINTED IN UNITED STATES

THIS PLANNER IS DESIGNED TO ASSIST AND SUPPORT SPECIAL EDUCATION TEACHERS IN THEIR DAILY PLANNING AND ORGANIZATION. THE AUTHOR, EMMA STINNETTE, HAS MADE EVERY EFFORT TO ENSURE THE ACCURACY OF THE INFORMATION WITHIN THIS PLANNER, BUT DISCLAIMS ANY LIABILITY FOR ERRORS OR OMISSIONS.

This Planner Belongs to

School

Grade Level

School Year

Student Meeting Dates

July	August	September
October	November	December
January	February	March
April	May	June

Related Services

Student	Related Service Providers

Contact Info

Student	Parent Contact Information

August

SUN	MON	TUES	WED	THURS	FRI	SAT

Back to School Activities

Rules & Routines

Week of ____________________

IEP

School

Life

Upcoming Meetings

Events & Appointments

August

SUN	MON	TUES	WED	THURS	FRI	SAT
○	○	○	○	○	○	○
○	○	○	○	○	○	○
○	○	○	○	○	○	○
○	○	○	○	○	○	○
○	○	○	○	○	○	○

Week of _______________________

IEP

School

Life

Upcoming Meetings

Events & Appointments

August

SUN	MON	TUES	WED	THURS	FRI	SAT

Week of _______________

IEP

School

Life

Upcoming Meetings

Events & Appointments

August

SUN	MON	TUES	WED	THURS	FRI	SAT

Week of _______________________________

IEP

School

Life

Upcoming Meetings

Events & Appointments

August

SUN	MON	TUES	WED	THURS	FRI	SAT

Week of ___________________

IEP

School

Life

Upcoming Meetings

Events & Appointments

August

SUN	MON	TUES	WED	THURS	FRI	SAT

September

SUN	MON	TUES	WED	THURS	FRI	SAT
○	○	○	○	○	○	○
○	○	○	○	○	○	○
○	○	○	○	○	○	○
○	○	○	○	○	○	○
○	○	○	○	○	○	○

Week of _______________________

IEP

School

Life

Upcoming Meetings

Events & Appointments

September

SUN	MON	TUES	WED	THURS	FRI	SAT

Week of __________________________________

IEP

School

Life

Upcoming Meetings

Events & Appointments

September

SUN	MON	TUES	WED	THURS	FRI	SAT
○	○	○	○	○	○	○
○	○	○	○	○	○	○
○	○	○	○	○	○	○
○	○	○	○	○	○	○
○	○	○	○	○	○	○

Week of ______________________________

IEP

School

Life

Upcoming Meetings

Events & Appointments

September

SUN	MON	TUES	WED	THURS	FRI	SAT

Week of ___________

IEP

School

Life

Upcoming Meetings

Events & Appointments

September

SUN	MON	TUES	WED	THURS	FRI	SAT

Week of _______________

IEP

School

Life

Upcoming Meetings

Events & Appointments

September

SUN	MON	TUES	WED	THURS	FRI	SAT

October

SUN	MON	TUES	WED	THURS	FRI	SAT

Week of _______________________

IEP

School

Life

Upcoming Meetings

Events & Appointments

October

SUN	MON	TUES	WED	THURS	FRI	SAT

Week of _______________

IEP

School

Life

Upcoming Meetings

Events & Appointments

October

SUN	MON	TUES	WED	THURS	FRI	SAT

Week of ___________________

IEP

School

Life

Upcoming Meetings

Events & Appointments

October

SUN	MON	TUES	WED	THURS	FRI	SAT

Week of _______________

IEP

School

Life

Upcoming Meetings

Events & Appointments

October

SUN	MON	TUES	WED	THURS	FRI	SAT

Week of ___________

JEP

School

Life

Upcoming Meetings

Events & Appointments

October

SUN	MON	TUES	WED	THURS	FRI	SAT

November

SUN	MON	TUES	WED	THURS	FRI	SAT
○	○	○	○	○	○	○
○	○	○	○	○	○	○
○	○	○	○	○	○	○
○	○	○	○	○	○	○
○	○	○	○	○	○	○

Week of ________________________________

IEP

School

Life

Upcoming Meetings

Events & Appointments

November

SUN	MON	TUES	WED	THURS	FRI	SAT

Week of ______________

IEP

School

Life

Upcoming Meetings

Events & Appointments

November

SUN	MON	TUES	WED	THURS	FRI	SAT

Week of _______________________

IEP

School

Life

Upcoming Meetings

Events & Appointments

November

SUN	MON	TUES	WED	THURS	FRI	SAT

Week of ____________________

JEP

School

Life

Upcoming Meetings

Events & Appointments

November

SUN	MON	TUES	WED	THURS	FRI	SAT

Week of _______________

Upcoming Meetings

Events & Appointments

December

SUN	MON	TUES	WED	THURS	FRI	SAT

Week of _______________

IEP

School

Life

Upcoming Meetings

Events & Appointments

December

SUN	MON	TUES	WED	THURS	FRI	SAT

Week of ________________________

JEP

School

Life

Upcoming Meetings

Events & Appointments

December

SUN	MON	TUES	WED	THURS	FRI	SAT

Week of ___________________

IEP

School

Life

December

SUN	MON	TUES	WED	THURS	FRI	SAT

Week of _______________________________

IEP

School

Life

Upcoming Meetings

Events & Appointments

December

SUN	MON	TUES	WED	THURS	FRI	SAT

Week of ________________________________

JEP

School

Life

Upcoming Meetings

Events & Appointments

December

SUN	MON	TUES	WED	THURS	FRI	SAT

January

SUN	MON	TUES	WED	THURS	FRI	SAT
◯	◯	◯	◯	◯	◯	◯
◯	◯	◯	◯	◯	◯	◯
◯	◯	◯	◯	◯	◯	◯
◯	◯	◯	◯	◯	◯	◯
◯	◯	◯	◯	◯	◯	◯

Week of ______________________

IEP

School

Life

Upcoming Meetings

Events & Appointments

January

SUN	MON	TUES	WED	THURS	FRI	SAT

Week of _______________

IEP

School

Life

Upcoming Meetings

Events & Appointments

January

SUN	MON	TUES	WED	THURS	FRI	SAT

Week of _______________

IEP

☐ _______________
☐ _______________
☐ _______________
☐ _______________
☐ _______________
☐ _______________
☐ _______________
☐ _______________
☐ _______________
☐ _______________

School

☐ _______________
☐ _______________
☐ _______________
☐ _______________
☐ _______________
☐ _______________
☐ _______________
☐ _______________
☐ _______________
☐ _______________

Life

☐ _______________
☐ _______________
☐ _______________
☐ _______________
☐ _______________
☐ _______________
☐ _______________
☐ _______________
☐ _______________
☐ _______________

Upcoming Meetings

○ _______________
○ _______________
○ _______________
○ _______________
○ _______________

Events & Appointments

○ _______________
○ _______________
○ _______________
○ _______________
○ _______________

January

SUN	MON	TUES	WED	THURS	FRI	SAT
○	○	○	○	○	○	○
○	○	○	○	○	○	○
○	○	○	○	○	○	○
○	○	○	○	○	○	○
○	○	○	○	○	○	○

Week of ____________________

<table>
<tr><td>

IEP

☐ ______________
☐ ______________
☐ ______________
☐ ______________
☐ ______________
☐ ______________
☐ ______________
☐ ______________
☐ ______________
☐ ______________
☐ ______________

</td><td>

School

☐ ______________
☐ ______________
☐ ______________
☐ ______________
☐ ______________
☐ ______________
☐ ______________
☐ ______________
☐ ______________
☐ ______________

</td><td>

Life

☐ ______________
☐ ______________
☐ ______________
☐ ______________
☐ ______________
☐ ______________
☐ ______________
☐ ______________
☐ ______________

</td></tr>
</table>

Upcoming Meetings

○ ______________
○ ______________
○ ______________
○ ______________
○ ______________

Events & Appointments

○ ______________
○ ______________
○ ______________
○ ______________
○ ______________

January

SUN	MON	TUES	WED	THURS	FRI	SAT
○	○	○	○	○	○	○
○	○	○	○	○	○	○
○	○	○	○	○	○	○
○	○	○	○	○	○	○
○	○	○	○	○	○	○

Week of _______________

IEP

School

Life

Upcoming Meetings

Events & Appointments

January

SUN	MON	TUES	WED	THURS	FRI	SAT

February

SUN	MON	TUES	WED	THURS	FRI	SAT
○	○	○	○	○	○	○
○	○	○	○	○	○	○
○	○	○	○	○	○	○
○	○	○	○	○	○	○
○	○	○	○	○	○	○

Week of __________________

<table>
<tr><td>

IEP

</td><td>

School

</td><td>

Life

</td></tr>
</table>

Upcoming Meetings

Events & Appointments

February

SUN	MON	TUES	WED	THURS	FRI	SAT

Week of ________________________

IEP

School

Life

Upcoming Meetings

Events & Appointments

February

SUN	MON	TUES	WED	THURS	FRI	SAT

Week of _______________________________

IEP

School

Life

SUN	MON	TUES	WED	THURS	FRI	SAT

Week of ______________________

IEP

School

Life

Upcoming Meetings

Events & Appointments

February

SUN	MON	TUES	WED	THURS	FRI	SAT

Week of ______________________

IEP

School

Life

Upcoming Meetings

Events & Appointments

February

SUN	MON	TUES	WED	THURS	FRI	SAT
○	○	○	○	○	○	○
○	○	○	○	○	○	○
○	○	○	○	○	○	○
○	○	○	○	○	○	○
○	○	○	○	○	○	○

March

SUN	MON	TUES	WED	THURS	FRI	SAT

Week of ____________________

IEP

School

Life

Upcoming Meetings

Events & Appointments

March

SUN	MON	TUES	WED	THURS	FRI	SAT

Week of ________________________

IEP

School

Life

Upcoming Meetings

Events & Appointments

March

SUN	MON	TUES	WED	THURS	FRI	SAT

Week of ______________________________

IEP

School

Life

Upcoming Meetings

Events & Appointments

March

SUN	MON	TUES	WED	THURS	FRI	SAT

Week of _______________________

IEP

School

Life

Upcoming Meetings

Events & Appointments

March

SUN	MON	TUES	WED	THURS	FRI	SAT

Week of _______________________

IEP

School

Life

Upcoming Meetings

Events & Appointments

March

SUN	MON	TUES	WED	THURS	FRI	SAT

April

SUN	MON	TUES	WED	THURS	FRI	SAT

Week of _______________

IEP

School

Life

Upcoming Meetings

Events & Appointments

April

SUN	MON	TUES	WED	THURS	FRI	SAT

Week of _______________________________

IEP

School

Life

Upcoming Meetings

Events & Appointments

April

SUN	MON	TUES	WED	THURS	FRI	SAT

Week of ________________________________

IEP

School

Life

Upcoming Meetings

Events & Appointments

April

SUN	MON	TUES	WED	THURS	FRI	SAT

Week of _______________________

IEP

School

Life

Upcoming Meetings

Events & Appointments

April

SUN	MON	TUES	WED	THURS	FRI	SAT

Week of _______________

IEP

School

Life

Upcoming Meetings

Events & Appointments

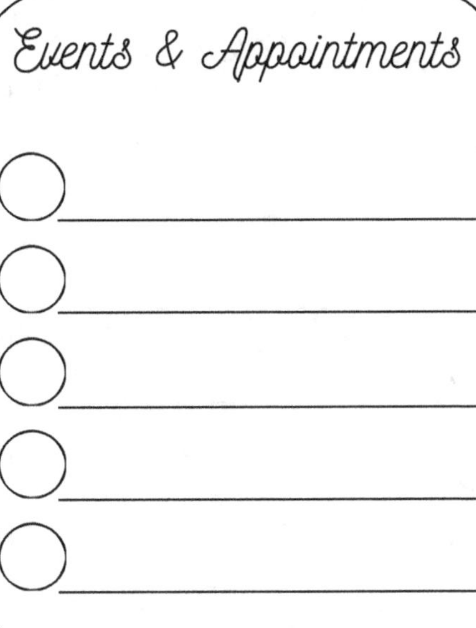

April

SUN	MON	TUES	WED	THURS	FRI	SAT

Week of ________________

IEP

School

Life

Upcoming Meetings

Events & Appointments

April

SUN	MON	TUES	WED	THURS	FRI	SAT

May

SUN	MON	TUES	WED	THURS	FRI	SAT

Week of ________________________________

IEP

School

Life

Upcoming Meetings

Events & Appointments

May

SUN	MON	TUES	WED	THURS	FRI	SAT

Week of _______________

IEP

School

Life

Upcoming Meetings

Events & Appointments

May

SUN	MON	TUES	WED	THURS	FRI	SAT

Week of ___________________

IEP

School

Life

Upcoming Meetings

Events & Appointments

May

SUN	MON	TUES	WED	THURS	FRI	SAT

Week of ___________________________

IEP

School

Life

Upcoming Meetings

Events & Appointments

May

SUN	MON	TUES	WED	THURS	FRI	SAT

Week of ___________________

JEP

School

Life

Upcoming Meetings

Events & Appointments

May

SUN	MON	TUES	WED	THURS	FRI	SAT

June

SUN	MON	TUES	WED	THURS	FRI	SAT
◯	◯	◯	◯	◯	◯	◯
◯	◯	◯	◯	◯	◯	◯
◯	◯	◯	◯	◯	◯	◯
◯	◯	◯	◯	◯	◯	◯
◯	◯	◯	◯	◯	◯	◯

Week of ________________________

IEP

School

Life

Upcoming Meetings

Events & Appointments

June

SUN	MON	TUES	WED	THURS	FRI	SAT

Week of _______________________________

IEP

School

Life

Upcoming Meetings

Events & Appointments

June

SUN	MON	TUES	WED	THURS	FRI	SAT

Week of

JEP

School

Life

Upcoming Meetings

Events & Appointments

June

SUN   MON   TUES   WED   THURS   FRI   SAT

Week of _______________________________

IEP

School

Life

Upcoming Meetings

Events & Appointments

June

SUN	MON	TUES	WED	THURS	FRI	SAT

Week of ______________________

IEP

School

Life

Upcoming Meetings

Events & Appointments

June

SUN	MON	TUES	WED	THURS	FRI	SAT

SUN	MON	TUES	WED	THURS	FRI	SAT
○	○	○	○	○	○	○
○	○	○	○	○	○	○
○	○	○	○	○	○	○
○	○	○	○	○	○	○
○	○	○	○	○	○	○

Week of _______________________________

IEP

School

Life

Upcoming Meetings

Events & Appointments

July

SUN	MON	TUES	WED	THURS	FRI	SAT

Week of ____________________

IEP

School

Life

Upcoming Meetings

Events & Appointments

July

SUN	MON	TUES	WED	THURS	FRI	SAT
○	○	○	○	○	○	○
○	○	○	○	○	○	○
○	○	○	○	○	○	○
○	○	○	○	○	○	○
○	○	○	○	○	○	○

Week of _______________________________

<table>
<tr><td>IEP</td><td>School</td><td>Life</td></tr>
</table>

IEP

School

Life

Upcoming Meetings

Events & Appointments

July

SUN	MON	TUES	WED	THURS	FRI	SAT

Week of _______________

IEP

School

Life

Upcoming Meetings

Events & Appointments

July

SUN	MON	TUES	WED	THURS	FRI	SAT

Week of ___________________________________

IEP

School

Life

Upcoming Meetings

Events & Appointments

July

SUN	MON	TUES	WED	THURS	FRI	SAT
○	○	○	○	○	○	○
○	○	○	○	○	○	○
○	○	○	○	○	○	○
○	○	○	○	○	○	○
○	○	○	○	○	○	○